MW01259211

Lines And Such As That.....

BY

Rufus Hagood Craig

ISBN: 1500223786
ISBN 13: 9781500223786
Library of Congress Control Number: 2014912457
CreateSpace Independent Publishing Platform
North Charleston, South Carolina

DEDICATION

TO

GERI ELLZEY CRAIG

ACKNOWLEDGMENT

I want to thank our dear friend Amanda Gunn for her creative spirit and technical expertise, without which, these lines would never have left their handwritten pages.

INTRODUCTION

Dear Reader,

I want to thank you for taking some of your valuable time to read these lines which I have penned, from time to time, over the past three decades. I have chosen these poems to be included in this collection, since they are the best of these lines which I have written; and they seem to be representative of my small body of work. I believe that my soul mate wife, Geri Ellzey Craig, (who is a talented author in her own right) is the only person who has read these poems in their entirety. She has encouraged me to share them with my family, friends, and those in the public who may have an interest. For her loving patience, kindness and encouragement, I dedicate this book to my dear wife. This encouragement of one, whose advice I admire and respect, is the primary reason for the public utterance of these very personal lines. My first grade teacher told my mother that I would not fully participate in "show and tell. " She said "Rufus will show, but he won't tell." Well today, I hope that I can prove that I can both show and tell.

Thank you again for your interest and I hope that your time and attention in reading these lines will have been well spent.

Rufus Hagood Craig
June 2014

BOOK DESCRIPTION

Lines And Such As That....is a collection of unique poetry that will light up your soul. This collection of forty three poems paints vibrant pictures of a journey through the author's life that is profoundly spiritual. Within the pages of this book, you find musings about mountain tops and valleys, sunrises and sunsets, and life's biggest and smallest events, as well as its unexpected gifts. Poems that celebrate the author's love for his wife convey romance and fun, expressing surprise and delight at a companionship filled with dancing, sandy beaches and family. Several poems are dedicated to 9/11, revealing his deep love of country, and many other poems speak reverently of his boundless wonder and love for God. Balancing the highs and lows of his more serious poems, he also offers whimsical verses evoking laughter and joy that provide respite from the pathos of his concern for hunger, poverty, and war in the world.

While each of Rufus Hagood Craig's poems capture feelings and emotions that are deeply personal, at the same time, this poetry collection gives voice to universal themes that speak to all of us.

TABLE OF CONTENTS

YOUR CALL

I wonder if you called, would I hear?
Perhaps you have, and I did not know.
I wonder if I could tune my ear,
To hear your call in the world's noise flow?

If I heard your call, what would I do?
If I heard your call, what would I say?
Would I leave my nets to follow you?
On my knees, would I begin to pray?

Are my bones too old to share one's load?
Have I lived too long to hear your call?
Not if I will walk your holy road.
Not if I will sing "You died for all."

Your call to me is ever so near.
I need only to give you my soul.
And when I hear, I will raise a cheer,
For that moment when I was made whole.

WHERE ARE THOSE

Where are those who inscribed our first rights
On timeless parchment for all to see?
Where are those who kindled the far lights
To freedom's way for those not yet free?

Where are the ones who bought early peace
For a price too dear for me to know?
Where are the ones who prayed wars would cease,
While defending the fields they would sow?

Where are those whose life blood was painted
In fetid swamps in some unknown land?
Where are those whose lives should be sainted,
As they are the reason we still stand?

Where are the ones who labored for naught,
In binding us close with new forged steel?
Where are the ones whose bodies were bought
And sold, as frontiers were brought to heel?

Where are the ones who would teach as one,
Bringing light to corners of the night?
Where are those who dreamed beyond the sun,
And solved the mystery of space flight?

The early ones have long slipped away;
But we should tread on their bones with care.
They teach the hard lessons for this day;
Which we must learn, and then we must share.

GOD'S ANCIENT PLAN

To watch alone as God's world awakes,
  And yawns to life in the early morn;
Reminds me that each of us partakes,
As His poetry once more is born.

The silent gull slipping out to sea,
Is colored by the burst of the sun;
Proclaiming each day a symphony
Of yet seen sights and songs to be sung.

There are times when I know you are near;
And your presence surely touches me.
These times are prints to keep and hold dear,
And to cherish for all times to be.

There is quiet for my noisy soul,
To be found as the earth stirs to life.
It's a gift to see God's dawn unfold,
As it has done through ages of strife.

I sometimes wonder when I should cease,
With these lines I pen from time to time.
And yet, God's ancient plan sings of peace,
Leading me once more to pray in rhyme.

FOR STRANGERS GONE
9-11-01

The weaver of all galaxies,
With love, kneels down to wipe our tears.
He soothes the souls of those he frees,
To fly to him on holy biers.

He hears our cries in the deep night,
For strangers gone before we met.
He sees our heartstrings wound so tight.
We pray our hearts won't break just yet.

The authors of death shall not rest;
Nor shall they ever receive peace.
May their dark souls never be blessed.
May they live our grief without cease.

Let not our pain obscure your will;
Lest our anger leads us to shame.
Please teach our sorrow to lie still;
And lead us to spread freedom's flame.

TIGER CAT

There's a tiger cat who comes around,
   Each afternoon on his daily round;
Hunting our birds, which always abound,
And then he leaves, as if none were found.

This life ritual occurs each day;
Unfolding as scenes in some stage play.
Our birds egg him on with songs so gay,
And play their parts in a time honed way.

He doesn't seem to be too depressed,
Over his constant lack of success.
Life's failures never leave him distressed.
Should his true feelings be second guessed?

I think I can learn from Tiger Cat.
If life conjures ways to knock me flat;
I should get up and dust off my hat.
If cats wore hats, Tiger would do that.

LONG PURPLE DRESSES

Now you can wear long purple dresses,
   And step out in high top tennis shoes:
Sport wild flower braids in your tresses,
While you and your man dispel the blues.

You can sip red dog and grin at life;
As your dear friends begin to wonder.
You can't erase all the pain and strife,
But your joy can rip them asunder.

To howl at the moon is not so bad;
If you can do it with your best friend.
What strikes me as being all too sad,
Is if you wait, will the moonlight end?

You seem to shuck those entwining chains,
That bind us to some wheel of duty.
I marvel at how life's fearsome rains,
Have molded you a work of beauty.

A SHARD

If I am a mere shard of we,
Then we and I must join as one.
But who will stop and succor me,
As I lie alone in the sun?

Do we need to stay connected
If we live in a walled off land?
How can our souls be perfected,
If you will not reach for my hand?

As one shard, I wait in the dust,
While my edges touch only space.
But if we're joined through love and trust,
We can start to see our Lord's face.

AFRICA CRIES

My brother's eyes closed before morn;
No longer will he fear the day.
My sister cries as the forlorn;
She no longer calls me to play.

My paper skin longs to reclaim
Its lost flesh, which once was robust.
Yet my tired lips still fail to name,
When they last touched other than dust.

Would that I could taste the sweet rain,
As it heals the wounds of our land.
Would that our souls could feel again,
The warmth of our lost brother's hand.

Do not wait silent for so long,
That our faint cries cannot be heard.
Do not wait til our final song
Is sung low by the mourning bird.

IF I

If I could fly your children to the portals of
beyond,
And trace the secret pathways of your mind;
If I could use the desert sands to feed the hungry
throng,
Am I greater than the best of all mankind?

If I could cover mountains with my treasures heaped
on high;
If I could scour the seas of their lost trove;
If I could soar higher than your holy angels' sky;
Am I too bright for your eyes to behold?

If I could but catch the stars and make them all stand
in line;
And teach them to dance til the dawn draws nigh;
If I could halt moments from ever being time;
Am I not crowned the highest of the high?

What do I gain if I can still strive to be;
And yet am deaf to the still small voice of thee?
For to dream only of what I will to be,
Blinds my eyes to your holy plan penned for me.

OUR CHILD

Starving young eyes, devoid of hope;
Hope is for those who live.
Her shrunken breast is always near.
She's gone; no more to give.
Now the eyes are grief and fear.

Sad, tired eyes close at last;
But for the want
Of a simple repast.

Kings and princes,
Posture and preen.
They promise salvation
For mankind supreme.
They protect the dignity
Of all human beings.

Sad, tired eyes close at last;
But for the want
Of a simple repast.

We pride ourselves
In our wonderful works.
To the moon,
And far beyond.
We harness great rivers;
Cure all our ills;
To every need we respond.

Sad, tired eyes close at last;
But for the want
Of a simple repast.

It makes little sense,
Since man is all great,
That starving children still die.
If we can make war,
In a manner ornate;
Why can't we heed a child's cry?

Sad, tired eyes close at last;
But for the want
Of a simple repast.

MY PATH

I pray to go out not knowing,
My path or where I am going.
I pray to go until I cease,
Asking if I should pray for peace.

I pray I quit my endless stream
Of reasons why I never seem,
To hear your angels' holy sound,
And follow them to where you're found.

I pray to live my life and do
Those things pleasing only to you.
I pray that when my days are known,
My path leads straightway to your throne.

TOGETHER

Together we built a mighty plane;
　　Made of tinker sticks and roundy things.
Its ray guns zizzled and shot pure flame;
As they zapped huge cyborgs with their zings.

To build it took less than an hour;
Yet its life was much longer than that.
We heard it cleared the Eiffel tower;
And saved mankind from zog's evil cat.

Together we filled a treasure chest,
With mind scenes which time cannot erase.
As we go our ways to seek life's quests,
May we always find that special place.

WINDS OF TIME

The winds of time blow hard on my face;
Swirling with old prints of yesteryear.
There we are dancing in our own space,
And learning to love all that is dear.

Images were strewn like grains of sand,
Into old crevices in my mind.
When retrieved, they show us hand in hand,
Learning our love was His gift to find.

We sought our love and all it could mean.
We found His love as he made us one.
He taught us that on Him we could lean;
In times when we fear we are alone.

We now approach a new span of time,
With open minds to all it could bring.
May we follow His bells as they chime.
May we some day with His angels sing.

CYRUS

Something told me his name was Cyrus.
Before we met, my body was well.
But he springs from some ancient virus;
And he was born to be my death knell.

Cyrus is happy if he can make
My lungs convulse and my fever soar.
If my body parts in concert ache,
He knows he's done what he came here for.

His moves reflect an NBA star.
Nothing can touch him or bring him low.
He pushes the limits of just how far,
My diseased body, in fact, can go.

His ancestors gave mankind bad flu;
Which did not help our fortunes to thrive.
They've lived well in the earth's molten stew:
Which tells me that Cyrus will survive.

Right now, I'm not so sure about me.

CLAY JARS

If we are but fragile jars of clay,
May your spirit in us overflow:
And quinch our souls who long for that day,
When you touch us all before we go.

Before we go, may you slack the thirst
Of those of us whose bones have gone dry.
Before we go, may we be immersed
In your love on which all can rely.

When my jar fills up with the world's cares,
And its water turns a brackish hue;
I still feel the touch of one whose prayers
Will forgive me for all that I do.

When I lose my way, I lose my sight
Of the right road, as laid out by you.
But my swamp dark slips off at first light,
If I can but keep your lamp in view.

Should I wonder if Christ's light will dim
If I wander off the beaten track?
Not if I hold close the print of Him,
Etched in his blood, as He leads me back.

THOUGHTS

You Are:
The passion of a lifetime,
    Spent in loving and caring;
Mixed with the sweet innocence
Of youth reborn and sharing.

I Love:
To watch red sunsets with you,
And the early gold sunrise;
And feel the wind on your face,
And taste salt on your lips and eyes.

You Are:
Hot coffee in the morning,
Under a slow ceiling fan,
Cheese Danish and funny hats,
The warmth of your nearby hand.

I Love:
Your warmth, your strength, your tears;
To hold you, and take away the hurt;
But most of all, to be near.

How many ways can I say "I Love you"?
The best is to hold you close,
Touch your soul,
Become one with you,
Pour tout les temps.

A CHRISTMAS TALE

This is a tale of that splendid night,
When shepherds came to see God's pure love.
Surely time stopped to witness the sight,
Of the birth of His son from above.

It is a tale of gifts for a king,
Proffered to a child on bended knee.
It is a tale of angels who sing
Of God's precious gift for you and me.

It is a tale of this newborn life,
Offering new life for all who come.
It tells of hope in the face of strife,
Given to us that night in His son.

It's a tale of our brokenness healed,
With the balm of God's redeeming grace.
It's a tale of our goodness revealed,
And our sadness banished with no trace.

Do I dare unwrap His holy gift?
I need only to open my soul;
And with cleansing love, He then will lift
Me as a child, and make me whole.

YOU

You are walking through mission filled times;
  You feel that your heart may overflow.
These days may lack the music of chimes;
But they whisper a song sweet and low.

A soul is nearing her journey's end;
With no one but you to pray her home.
You care for her as her only friend;
And show her where the angels have flown.

There is a holy hand guiding you,
As you pray for God's will to be done.
His healing balm covers you anew;
As she draws near to the Holy One.

Before the stars were placed far above,
He knew when this chapter would unfold:
And that you would teach her of His love,
And of His grace so long ago told.

I thank God for our souls joined as one,
In those days before the sun was born.
I thank God for our lives joined as one;
Which I celebrate on each new morn.

GULLS

Cold, gray mist creeps in at dawn;
Gulls in communion on the sand.
Battle lines are discussed and drawn;
Silent contemplation of their windward plan.

The dawn melts into glorious day:
Once more they take to the skies.
A target is spotted, into the fray;
Their screeches sound the battle cry.

Wheeling and diving in mad delight;
Soon, sanity flees the flock.
The silvery school whets their appetite:
On land, they regroup and take stock.

This winged flock feeding ritual,
Repeats in man each day.
We laud ourselves for being spiritual;
Yet, truly, we adore the fray.

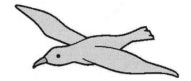

TWENTY FIVE

My muse, once again, has lost his way.
He has been mute for more than a while:
Leaving me void in what I should say,
As I create in my museless style.

But I find the words flow from my pen,
When I consider my life with you.
My old box of lines sits wide open,
As I select from the tried and true.

We have walked some roads not found on maps.
We have lived through times only we share.
I know in my heart, with no perhaps,
I was made whole through your love and prayer.

We fast danced close when the sun was high,
And slow danced close to the night bird's song.
Our days reached for the top of the sky.
We begged our nights to go on and on.

We have loved long, and I hope loved well;
Even though we've slogged through heavy seas.
If we did good, only time will tell:
But my bet is that we're the bees knees.

The years have flown on swift eagle's wings,
And our love deepens as each slips by.
Would that we dance 'til the last dove sings,
And the moon goes dark in the night sky.

JIM

When the sun fails to ever arise,
I know soul deep you will light the way.
When your birds seem to have left the skies,
I know soul deep they will fly some day.

When my feet can find no easy ground,
I know soul deep you will carry me.
When time has erased even his sound,
Still, I will know that he is home free.

When my heart pieces lie in a heap,
I know you will help me sort them out.
I know you will show me how to keep
Them together, as life goes about.

I know these things for you have told me,
That you walk with me this unknown road.
He is gone, yet I know we will be
Joined once again in your high abode.

TREMONT

Built with love and care ages ago:
Heart pine floors hewn perfect by hand.
Graceful lines took shape, ever so slow.
When finished, her essence bespoke grand.

Her full life beheld a time gone by.
A time to touch, and pause to reflect.
Sundowns spent in banter and reply.
A time to care for those we neglect.

Sunshine washes her elegant halls.
She knows laughter and tears from the past.
Did she hear music from festive balls?
Did she learn of loves and dreams held fast?

All too soon, old age took its sad toll.
Her mistress gone, with no one to care.
The grand era had played out its role.
Slow decay was her everyday fare.

Brought back by loving hands who knew her.
Restored to elegance with rare skill.
Will her rebirth foretell an era,
Of love and peace from living God's will?

Our lives, as hers, are restored with love.
To God we owe thanks for this blessing.
May our home reflect the peaceful dove;
And God's radiant love increasing.

HIS

His whisper begged for water,
 And I told him 'not today'.
His tired eyes wept for mercy;
But I passed along my way.

He left my mind as quickly,
As the twilight sun's last ray.
But he was there when I fell.
How he knew, I cannot say.

His thin arms could but hold me;
As he tried to ease my pain.
My burden was so heavy,
Yet for him he showed no strain.

His eyes bespoke his hunger,
Which had come to be his friend.
Still he fed me with his heart.
His grace seemed never to end.

YOU AND I

We've travelled some miles, you and I:
And kicked a few shells in the sand.
We've searched for lost stars in the sky;
And we've danced to a fifties band.

We've heard the low moan of a storm,
As it crashed upon our own beach.
Your touch has always kept me warm:
Your eyes have held me in their reach.

Time has passed on since we began.
It eased on by; was lost in space.
He gave us years to live His plan.
He honed your beauty with His grace.

We'll travel more roads, you and I.
We've not danced the last of this dance.
We have more time to laugh and cry;
To live with no love left to chance.

CROSS OF HOPE
9-11-01

*T*he rubble from that fateful day,
   Still smolders from their unspent hate.
And yet, they failed to have their way.
Their will cannot decide our fate.

Your will guides us through bitter rain,
Of our sad tears which soak your earth.
You hold us close, and ease our pain;
And fill us with songs of rebirth.

It emerged from the twisted steel;
A symbol of abiding grace.
Your cross of hope will always heal;
And lead us to your holy place.

MAY I

May I turn to you,
As I seek my way;
In all the seconds
Of every day:
My loving father,
This I pray.

May I live my life
In your holy way:
And at the nightfall
Of my final day;
May I be with you
This I pray.

THOUGHTS AT THE BEACH

There's a quiet time in the morning,
   When I almost hear the earth revolve.
If I'm still, doves begin their mourning;
And frets soon lose their need to resolve.

I can come to you, and when I pray,
I know secret dreams are heard by you.
You've known for all time what I would say,
As I lift my faith to you anew.

When the sun rises from the deep sea,
How far will it journey by night's reach?
For a child, there is a need to see
Beyond wet morning sands at the beach.

My grandchild's quest for knowledge and truth,
Flow from deep within in constant streams.
My wisdom falls short of certain proof,
And yet, may I help build early dreams.

May I begin to pass on to them,
The song of a granddad's love and grace;
Of how your bright light will never dim,
Through the myriad turns of life's race.

THANKSGIVING

If I give thanks, without then giving
Your gifts to those whose feet go unshod;
Am I a man of thankful living,
Walking the path where the saints have trod?

If I give without a thankful heart,
Your gifts to a child barely living;
Can I claim I have made a new start,
Toward a life lived in thanksgiving?

I think that I may have missed the point;
As I failed to learn thanks filled giving:
Thanks and giving should fit as a joint;
Without both, where is the thanksgiving?

FEED YOUR SHEEP

Will you teach me how to feed your sheep,
When my cupboard seems to be too bare?
Are there certain rules that I must keep,
To learn, with grace, to love and to share?

How can I know which sheep I should feed,
If their cries cry loud and drown all thought?
Will you show me those sheep most in need,
And who should be fed with food I brought?

If I feel the need to feed your lost,
Should I act on that and nothing more?
Should I move the mountains at all costs,
Or pray and wait for some open door?

Do I have more "should I's" than I should?
I think my "I wills" are far too few.
Perhaps I should not ask "how I could";
But just feed your sheep and follow you.

MASQUES

I don't remember where I found it.
It stayed hidden for years from my view.
I tried it on, but it would not fit,
As once it had, before there was you.

While worn by me, it had covered my
Sadness and deep fears, mixed with still rage.
Its self-sure, keen wit would keep my cry
Of anguish well hidden from life's stage.

I can't recall why I put it on.
Young children, I've noticed, don't wear them.
Perhaps life's pain causes us to don
Our masks to conceal out hurt within.

Have I gained by removing my shield,
Permitting my soul's core to be seen?
Should the naked review by all yield
Deep wisdom, with a full life serene?

I think not, from the life role I've played
Since the Lord taught me to laugh and cry.
But to feel love, where feelings were stayed,
Is a Holy gift gold cannot buy.

We build walls and wear masks to hide pain,
And to distance us from those who plead.
Yet our Lord died to remove our stain,
Can we refuse to love those in need?

TOO YOUNG

They are too young, and yet they still fall;
In distant places with names so strange.
Our young always have answered our call;
When we've run amok and will not change.

Is there some ancient cosmic mandate,
That wars must be waged with untried youth?
Try as we may, we cannot create
One peaceful day built on trust and truth.

If called, they will come until that day,
There are none left to send out to fall.
And on that day, if wars have their way,
Old men will have to answer the call.

YOUR MIND

*B*efore the first peaks arose,
At the dawning of your time:
You knew you would hold me close,
At my evensong's last chime.

When you formed the grains of earth,
And the seeds they would surround;
You knew my first cry at birth,
And my joy when you were found.

You were all when time began,
Yet you know each wayward thought.
You hold me when I cannot stand,
And forgive the pain I've wrought.

To know your mind is fool's play;
I cannot and will not try.
I know your love is my stay.
It's peace I cannot deny.

GOOD TIMES

It's hard to believe another year
Has eased right on by into our past.
If we're real still, we almost can hear
Next year bearing down on us too fast.

Last year's good times were just ours to share.
We hid them in our hidey hole.
And when our good times cupboard runs bare,
They'll be unearthed, relived and retold.

Each year with you is a special gift;
Filled with your beauty and graceful ways.
May we always be able to sift
For life's gold for the rest of our days.

HEART SONGS

Do heart songs sung soft at eventide,
Disappear beyond my line of sight?
Or, on unborn waves, do their thoughts ride,
To grace distant shores by end of night?

My heart songs for you can fill the skies,
And cover you up like morning dew.
I've crafted lines to laud your fine eyes,
And I'll sing new songs touching just you.

But lines are just meager words at best.
Scriven with some hope to touch your heart.
I hope my heart songs will stand time's test,
And will live in you when we're apart.

BEYOND

If I could see beyond my sight,
Would I view your face each day?
If I could reach beyond my grasp,
Would you never slip away?

If I could hear beyond the wind,
Would you whisper in the night?
If I could feel beyond a touch,
Would you soothe me, oh so light?

If I could run beyond the sun,
Would you stay the course with me?
If I could sail beyond the charts,
Would you join me on the sea?

Alone, I know I'll never find,
Those dreams I so long to share.
Together we can fly beyond,
And follow our dreams we dare.

THOSE NOW LEFT BEHIND

I beg you not to leave me,
For I have not learned your ways.
If you go, I will not know
Where your secret knowledge stays.

I can't teach my soon born child,
To ponder your reach of mind:
If my path leads not to you,
But to those now left behind.

May I learn to teach my child,
About brave lives and lost stars.
May I live to see the day
When knowledge removes his scars.

How can I find your treasure
Of wisdom, if you depart?
How can I ever share it
If I cannot touch your heart?

LONG LOVE

Try as I might, the words seem to fail
To fly off my pen and land in place.
My ship of new lines never sets sail,
And is mired down in silent disgrace.

And if my mind has taken a yen,
To wander off in my time of need;
I still write of your three score and ten,
And how you've touched each thought, word and
deed.

My love for you has grown more on more;
Yet good times gone are hard to replace.
For us, I wish that I could restore
Halcyon days to fill up our space.

In this, the autumn of life, I find,
As soul mates, we still stroll down the road.
This gift of long love is far too kind;
For together we lighten our load.

Would that you could lead me on and on,
Beyond this life and into His light.
Would that you could help me hear His song,
As He calls from the far side of night.

FOLLOW ME

He said "follow me", and I asked where?
Just follow me, for you know the way.
Should I follow you into thin air?
Just follow me, for I am the way.

But how can I stop and follow you,
If my needs are great, as you well know?
I knew your cares before you were you.
Just follow me, we have miles to go.

So I will follow Him where He goes;
Until all of my seconds have passed.
For He, alone, is the one who knows,
How many steps our journey will last.

COME WITH ME

We have had a journey, you and I;
Our pathway filled with crannies and nooks.
We have sailed beyond the azure sky,
Where pirates abound with snarls and hooks.

We have danced to tunes of highland elves,
And have battled long to save the day.
In time's mist we have lost ourselves,
Only to be found and shown the way.

The road for us is always unknown,
But we know that it is well laid out.
We have many miles yet to be flown.
Of this, I am sure, there is no doubt.

So come with me, and let's find that place,
Where we are led next to feed His sheep,
So walk with me, and let us embrace,
Those visions He gave us both to keep.

THE RIGHT ROAD

*I*f I have lost my way home to you;
   Your hand has led me to your right road.
When my time worn swamps beckon anew,
You will guide me to your high abode.

I may not know when my steps have strayed,
But your spirit is ever with me.
It points me to the road you have laid,
For my journey to your Holy See.

You built us the right road to follow.
It is found in your sacred pages.
The calls of other roads ring hollow,
Compared to your road for all ages.

LOOSE BONES

I once was robust and filled with life.
My bounty of good things knew no end.
But then I was called a friend of strife.
As I lost all on which I depend.

I have become a bag of loose bones;
Tied together with old string and wire.
I cannot hear the earth's ancient tones;
Nor can I feel the sun's warming fire.

The soil is bare and no longer feeds
Those who seek sustenance from the ground.
I dined this morning on my last seeds,
And cried out for help, but none was found.

But you heard my cry and calmed my fears.
You loosened my chains to set me free.
As your spirit wiped clean all my tears,
I knew then you would never leave me.

WILL YOU

Will you till those fields where I need you,
    And work the hard earth I call my own?
Will you seek me in all that you do,
And walk with me when you are alone?

Will you touch the ones the world won't see,
And hold them close as their end draws near?
If asked, will you do these things for me,
Or will you cling to ways you hold dear?

Will you walk with me the unknown road,
And know, soul deep, that I walk with you?
Will you ease the widow's heavy load,
And bring hope to those whose hopes are few?

Will you succor those whose lives are dry,
And whose days go on for far too long?
Will you wipe the tear in my child's eye,
Who nightly weeps for a mother's song?

Will you walk with me when no one knows?
Will you walk with me when no one cares?
Will you help me open hearts that close?
Will you light the way to Heaven's stairs?

ABOUT THE AUTHOR

Rufus Hagood Craig is a retired corporate attorney who spent the majority of his legal career in the forest products industry. Now he devotes his time to his family, his church, and the joyful pursuit of various retirement projects. He resides in Montgomery, Alabama, with his wife, Geri Ellzey Craig, an accomplished author of a number of books and short stories. The Craigs are dedicated members of the First United Methodist Church.

With the loving encouragement of his wife, Craig published his first book of poetry, Lines And Such As That…. In this collection he shares his reflections and inspirations arising from his life's journey through the past thirty years.

Rufus Hagood Craig celebrates the publication of this book of poetry in loving memory of his son, Dr. James Stuart Craig, who passed away on August 29, 2012.

Made in the USA
San Bernardino, CA
24 August 2014